The World's Greatest Composers

Antonio Vivaldi

by Pam Brown

OTHER TITLES IN THE SERIES
Ludwig van Beethoven by Pam Brown (1-85015-302-7)
John Lennon by Michael White (1-85015-304-3)
Wolfgang Amadeus Mozart by Michael White
   (1-85015-300-0)
Peter Ilych Tchaikovsky by Michael Pollard (1-85015-303-5)
Coming Soon
Johann Sebastian Bach by Christopher Gibb (1-85015-311-6)
Frederic Chopin (1-85015-310-8)
Bob Marley (1-85015-312-4)

Picture Credits:
AGK: 16, 25, 34, 36, 41; Bridgeman Art Library: 4, 23, 26, 44-5; Christie's Colour Library: 12; Mary Evans Picture Library: 6; Explorer: 27; Gamma: 33 (top); Giraudon: 21; Image Bank: 13, 55; Image Select: 11, 14, 37; London Features International: 58; The Photo Co-op: 60; Scala: 8-9, 22, 30, 40, 48; Sotheby's: 37; Spectrum Colour Library: 33 (below), 50 (both); Zefa: 5, 51, 54, 59.

Published in Great Britain in 1992
by Exley Publications Ltd,
16 Chalk Hill, Watford,
Herts WD1 4BN, United Kingdom.

Copyright © Exley Publications, 1992
Copyright © Pam Brown, 1991

A copy of the CIP data is available from
the British Library on request

ISBN 1-85015-301-9

All rights reserved. No part of this publication may be reproduced or transmitted in any form or by any means, electronic or mechanical, including photocopy, recording or any information storage and retrieval system without permission in writing from the Publisher.

Series editor: Helen Exley
Editorial: Samantha Armstrong and Margaret Montgomery
Picture editor: Alex Goldberg of Image Select
Typeset by Brush Off Studios, St Albans.
Printed by Cambus Litho, East Kilbride.

Antonio VIVALDI

Pam Brown

Beginnings

We are in the country that would later become known as Italy – but which, in this year of 1678, is still a hotchpotch of little city states – each jealous of the other.

It is a bright May morning, the wide waters of Venice's *Canale di San Marco* dancing with sunlight, the sky without a cloud. A small group of people are hurrying in the direction of the church of San Giovanni in Bragura, threading their way through the familiar alley-ways, passing from shadow to sun as they cross the little side canals. The narrow streets are hung about with washing, the window-sills bright with pots of flowers – and from those windows women call to one another and to passers-by.

Someone is singing and the song is taken up by a boatman, to echo and re-echo against the peeling stucco of the houses.

And so the newborn baby, Antonio Lucio Vivaldi, goes to be received into the Church. He is wrapped up tightly against the shining air, for he is not strong and was christened the moment he was born – by the midwife, who feared he could not live. He goes with the sound of Venice in his ears – and that is the sound of music.

Antonio Vivaldi, who would grow to become one of the world's greatest composers, was the first child of Giovanni Battista and Camilla Calicchio Vivaldi. Giovanni earned his money as a barber, but his roots were in Breschia, a town famous for its violin makers, and he himself was a violinist of growing reputation.

There were to be five more children, but only Antonio inherited Giovanni's gift for music – along with his red hair.

Opposite: The people of Venice delighted in their city and loved pageantry. Here they attend a gondola race – wearing the cloaks and the masks of Carnival. The elaborately-decorated gondolas are moored along the banks, each vying with the other in grandeur and ingenuity. Below: Every view of the entrance to Venice's Grand Canal is dominated by the magnificent church of Santa Maria della Salute. The same view dominated Venice during Vivaldi's life – and the entire city was central to his music.

"La Serenissima"

Antonio Vivaldi was born on March 4, 1678 – the day an earthquake shook the city of Venice – in a house tucked away in the confusion of waterways and alleys that lay behind the naval dockyard, the *Arsenale*. It was the biggest dockyard in the world and for centuries, it had been the heart of Venetian prosperity. From here had come the ships of war and commerce that had made Venice mistress of the trade routes, powerful and rich beyond belief. In the fifteenth century she had been the envy of the known world – *La Serenissima*, the Most Serene Republic. But there had been bitter wars and plots, that had led to an ugliness beneath the grandeur – betrayal, spies, arrests and sudden executions.

Venice had been a country that had stood against the Pope, against Spain, against the Turks – but the cost had been great. Ten years before Vivaldi's birth Venice had lost Crete – her most valued colony. Thirty thousand Venetians had been killed in the last gallant defence. And Venice had faced bankruptcy. After centuries of power, *La Serenissima* had tasted humiliation.

At the height of Venice's power, at the beginning of the fifteenth century, ships were built and fitted out here at the "Arsenale". It formed the heart of Venice's domination of the trade routes. But when Vivaldi was born the city's importance had severely diminished and the once busy dockyards lay almost silent.

The *Arsenale* no longer echoed to the noise of ship building. The workforce had dwindled, for new sea routes were opening up and trade was passing into other hands.

Another city might have gone down into obscurity, but Venice possessed a vibrant life that could not be dulled or drowned. If Venice had once been obsessed by wealth and trade and power she had, at the same time, loved ceremonial, magnificent art and architecture – and music. These remained.

As the old priorities faded, so Venice would give herself over to pleasure. Toward the end of Vivaldi's life there would be peace and, without the financial burden of war, Venice would find a new role.

Antonio was born at the moment when Venice was changing, in her own eyes and the eyes of the world. These sunset years were to have a vivid life of their own – and Antonio was to play a vital part in them.

> *"Venice and Vivaldi, the two words are closely linked in the mind but Venice is a curiosity, magical but ghostly, a jewelled and fantastic relic, while Vivaldi's music is vibrant, surging with life and energy, as passionate and compelling as when it first echoed in the city of the sea."*
>
> John Booth, from his biography, "Vivaldi".

The Vivaldis and Venice

Antonio's father, Giovanni Vivaldi, was becoming recognized as a violinist of extraordinary skill. By the time his son was seven, Giovanni was no longer a barber who played the violin. He was a violinist to the ducal chapel of San Marco, the very heart of the city's music. He was referred to in its register as "Rossi", the red-haired. Venice was greedy for music and valued such people for their virtuosity – even though she despised their lack of rank.

Recognizing Antonio's talent, Giovanni had taken his son's musical education in hand. The boy was quick to learn – both from his father and the other leading musicians of San Marco. He made rapid progress, so much so that before he was thirteen, he was considered good enough to deputize for his father in his absence.

Antonio Vivaldi took lessons, walking from his home the short distance to the great central church of Venice, San Marco. He delighted in the sights, the sounds, the excitement of his city, the strangely luminous air, the ever-present glimmer of water.

Wherever he went, music found him. Even the

It was from trading on the sea that Venice had won all her glory. So, every year, the leader of the city, the Doge, would head a grand ceremony to wed Venice to the sea with a golden ring. There would be much music and loud cheering following the huge procession of decorated boats gliding out into the sea.

workers sang – some in voices that challenged those of opera singers in power and beauty.

Visitors were astounded by the way the people sang as they went about their daily chores. A builder or storekeeper sang and others took up the tune, singing parts as if they were trained musicians.

Even the little bands that played under the hotel windows were both talented and skilled.

A rich heritage

Venice was a most wonderful city in which to grow up. Built upon islands, interlaced with waterways, its squares and alleys linked with hundreds of

bridges, it offered a child endless surprises – markets, sideshows, processions....

The Grand Canal was lined with the palaces of the wealthy. Great churches towered above their own reflections – and within them were most wonderful pictures, glowing clear and bright – paintings by the masters of the past, Giorgione, Titian, Bellini and Veronese – and by the new artists, Tiepolo and Canaletto.

By day and by night the gondolas – beautiful flat-bottomed craft unique to Venice – passed and repassed – wedding parties, solemn funerals taking the dead to their own silent island, people on business, traders, tourists, all the world it seemed.

> "The Piote of the Signora Mocenigo represented the Chariot of the Night drawn by four sea horses, and shewing the rising of the moon, accompanied by the stars, the statues on each side representing the hours to the number of twenty-four, rowed by gondoliers in rich liveries, which were changed three times, all of equal richness and the decorations changed also to the dawn of Aurora and the midday sun, the statues being new dressed every time, the first in green, the second red, and the last blue, all equally laced in silver, there being three races."
>
> Lady Mary Montague, writing about a gondola race, 1740.

> "These extremely interesting years at the close of a century that had produced so many new forms, while still more were being elaborated, were the years of Vivaldi's youth. With alert intelligence, he took up the influences that were crowding in on him and by the strength of his originality, developed them beyond Corelli and Torelli."
>
> Walter Kolneder, from "Antonio Vivaldi, His Life and Work".

The gondoliers sang, as all Venice sang. The German writer Goethe described how on a calm, starlit night their songs would take on a new beauty. One would begin a song and from far off, across the wide canal, another would take up the answering verse – their voices clear in the silence, amplified to a ghostly resonance by the waters between them. Sometimes the singers held their audiences entranced all through a summer night.

The canals were the perfect setting for pageantry – and for regattas, when extravagantly-decorated gondolas raced the length of the Grand Canal.

The most splendid and significant of Venetian ceremonies took place once a year in spring. Then the chief magistrate, the elected leader of Venice, the Doge, was escorted aboard the carved and gilded barge of state. Accompanied by the boats of the nobility and a vast swarm of gondolas, the Doge and his dignitaries were rowed down the Grand Canal to the sound of music and trumpets ... out to the sea. There, with great solemnity, the Doge cast a golden ring into the waters, a symbol of the marriage of Venice to the sea, the source of her glory.

From every vantage point ashore the people of Venice watched the fleet of boats go by, delighting in this celebration of the magnificence of their city – even though the great days were past.

And young Antonio was there, turning the glory and the glitter, the trumpets and the voices, to music in his head. He took in this extraordinary mixture and stored it away.

Even now, three hundred years later, we can hear the combination of grandeur and light-heartedness that was Venice, in Antonio Vivaldi's music.

"Il Prete Rosso" – the red-headed priest

Giovanni Vivaldi's work at San Marco meant that he got to know many important men among the clergy. The priesthood then was one of the few opportunities for advancement and was often regarded as a way to get on in the world. Despite Antonio's great musical gifts he was from a very

ordinary background and it must have seemed to the family that his best chance was to become a priest. Accordingly, on September 18, 1693, when Antonio Vivaldi was fifteen and a half, he received the tonsure, the symbolic shaving of a small circular patch from the crown of the head. This was the first step to becoming a priest. From what was written of him later in life he seems to have been genuinely religious and to have brought piety rather than cynicism to his new career.

He was not shut off from music. The churches were the very heart of music making, each vying with the other in its performance. Out of the candlelit darkness, the glitter of mosaic, the gleam of gold and the solemnity of ritual, the voices soared and whispered in San Marco. Even in the little churches, hidden among the city's network of canals, the beauty of the music could so move the heart, it is said, that some would cry out in wonder – or even faint from excess of emotion.

The church of San Marco is at the very heart of Venice. Vivaldi lived most of his life in this densely-populated part of the city. It is possible that he was trained by the choir master of the church and he definitely knew the music of San Marco as he once deputized for his father, Giovanni, there.

Vivaldi took ten years to train as a priest, much longer than usual, perhaps because music had become increasingly important to him. Although he only fulfilled his priesthood for a year, the Church inspired him to compose many beautiful pieces.

It took ten years – far longer than usual – for Antonio to work through the stages of his training for the priesthood. Unlike other students he did not go to college but worked as assistant in various churches and, probably by special dispensation, lived at home. He already had problems with his health and, no doubt, these hindered his progress, but music was filling his head. The violin and composition were inclined to edge theology out of his mind and take up a great deal of his time and energies.

On March 23, 1703 Antonio Vivaldi was ordained priest. He was now able to take his full role in church, but people who loved gossip said that he would leave the altar to scribble down a theme that had come into his head – and then return to complete the service.

But Vivaldi himself declared, later in life, that he had been driven to break off by his illness. He only acted as a full priest for one year. Then he had to discontinue, "having on three occasions had to leave the altar without completing it because of the ailment."

We do not know for certain what the illness was, but it was probably either asthma or a heart condition. It was to haunt him for the rest of his life – even though that life was to be one of extraordinary creativity and energy.

The Pietà

So, here was Antonio Vivaldi, twenty-five years old and a priest, but a priest of little use in religious ceremonies.

His life so far had fed Antonio's natural talent. Surrounded from the first by music and musicians, he had become an outstandingly brilliant violinist and spent more and more time composing. He only needed one golden opportunity to launch him upon his life's work. That opportunity came with his appointment in 1703 to teach the violin at the girls' orphanage to which he was to be linked for the next forty years of his life, the *Seminario musicale dell'Ospedale della Pietà*.

The Pietà, or orphanage, was one of four such

A modern view of Venice. The front of the Pietà has been completely rebuilt since Vivaldi's day, and the canal-side walk has changed – but we can still imagine him walking to work over the bridges watching the busy life of the great waterways. The waterbus has largely taken the place of the gondola as the usual method of transport.

institutions in Venice. They had been set up three hundred years before to cope with the problem of abandoned and otherwise homeless children. There was none of the help we expect today – and so they were left – the babies in a "convenient little space" between grating and wall, to be brought up by the nuns.

Once these establishments had been little more than refuges, but by Antonio Vivaldi's day, they had become far more. The emphasis in all the Ospedali was on music. Only girls were raised in them now – and those who showed musical talent, the *figli de coro* (the choir daughters) were given an exceptional musical training. The others, the *figli di commun* (the daughters of the community) were

> *"I vow to you that there is nothing so diverting as the sight of a young and pretty nun in white habit, with a bunch of pomegranate blossoms over her ear, conducting the orchestra and beating time with all the grace and precision imaginable."*
>
> Charles de Brosses, a historian, writing about the music of the Ospedali.

given a general schooling. There were about a thousand girls at the Pietà, during Vivaldi's time there.

Vivaldi's position as a priest and a violinist made him the obvious choice to teach in such an establishment. The orphanages were expensive to run, despite charitable and state donations, and most of the money for their upkeep came from concerts given by the pupils. All four Ospedali were rivals in excellence and each had built up a devoted following of musical enthusiasts. To many they were known as "nightingale cages".

Long before Vivaldi took up his post at the Pietà, its music was famous. One visitor wrote that the girls: "sing like nightingales and play the violin, flute, the organ, the oboe, the cello and the bassoon; in short, there is no instrument, however unwieldy, that can frighten them."

*In Vivaldi's day, the violin was much as we know it now. In England, the tiny fiddles were called "kits". Dancing masters carried them in the pockets of their skirted coats to accompany their lessons.
1,2. Pocket violins, 3. Treble violin, 4. Standard Treble violin, 5. Tenor violin,
6. Bass viol,
7. A "Trumscheit",
8. A "Scheidholst".*

Violin teacher

Antonio Vivaldi took up his position under the *maestro di coro,* Francesco Gasparini, and was to prove an excellent teacher. He found at his disposal a great range of musical talent in instrumentalists, soloists and chorus. It was as if he had been given a workshop, a laboratory, in which to try out and perfect his skills of composition.

The Pietà specialized in the use of unusual instruments, perhaps as a novelty to attract concert-goers. The experience was to give Vivaldi the ability to compose for a far wider range of instruments than other musicians of his day, and in entirely new combinations. It also taught him to write fine music for the ordinary performer as well as for the virtuoso. Working so closely with the girls he was to grow in understanding of the capabilities of specific instruments and voices.

Vivaldi's stunning violin performances attracted visitors to the Pietà. This made him very important to the Pietà because these concerts were run to raise money to pay for the care of the girls. He also taught the violin and supervised the purchase of instruments, and he acted as *maestro de concerti* whenever necessary, directed and played in orchestral performances and composed pieces as and when they were needed. Tourists from across Europe visited Venice especially to attend the Ospedali concerts – and the Pietà, under Vivaldi's influence, would become the high point of their stay.

Life at the Pietà

In another country an orphanage might have been a place of gloom and privation, but this was Venice. Even her convents were places of laughter and chatter and frequent visitors. It was scarcely accepted piety – but it was very Venetian.

In performance the young ladies were half-hidden from their audience in a gallery, behind a "lattice of ironwork", which added to the fascination of the concerts. After the concerts, the privileged could be introduced to them, and many girls married well.

"The combination of the gifted and spirited pupils of the Pietà and the gifted and furiously energetic young composer, who was only about twenty-five when he first took up his duties there, produced music that is characterized by an irrepressible energy and vitality, music which must have delighted the hearts of the young players as much as it enraptured the audience."

John Booth, from his biography, "Vivaldi".

"... certainly their churches are frequented more to please the ear than for real devotion."

Von Poellnitz, writing about the Ospedali.

The Pietà was considered by most to be the best of the Ospedali. The girls were of outstanding natural ability and Vivaldi improved on that to such an extent that the Pietà became famous all over Europe. Tourists would flock to see the girls perform. A screen in front of them added to the mystery.

The most talented senior girls were given the title of *Maestra* (Mistress), and were known by their Christian names, linked to their instruments, with very pleasing effect: Maestra Silvia dal Violino; Maestra Luciana Organista; Maestra Michieletta del Violin.

The organization of the Pietà was efficient and extremely democratic. The *figli di coro* were treated with great care and respect. If they were ill, they could be sent to the countryside to recuperate. If they felt the cold, they could apply for extra fuel. In turn, the older girls taught the younger, and the most senior also had considerable authority over the teachers. They had to sign the accounts each quarter to certify that their instructors had fulfilled their duties satisfactorily. They were paid more than Vivaldi himself.

Composer

Antonio Vivaldi's star was rising ... at first, it was his mastery of the violin that caught the public's attention. His technique dazzled all who heard him play.

Johan Friedrich von Uffenbach, architect and musician, wrote: "Vivaldi performed a solo accompaniment admirably, and at the end he added an improvised cadenza that quite confounded me, for such playing has not been heard before and can never be equalled. He placed his fingers but a hair's breadth from the bridge so that there was hardly room for the bow. He played thus on all four strings, with imitations and at unbelievable speed."

However, in 1705, it was Vivaldi's work as a composer that reached out beyond the performances at the Pietà. His first published music appeared – a collection of trio sonatas. Up to this point, his work had been known in its religious setting. Much of his church work is deeply peaceful. But now the lively, individual style for which we know Vivaldi today, became known to Italy, and indeed Europe.

It was usual to dedicate a composition to someone of rank and influence, with suitable humility. Vivaldi's dedication was a model of self-deprecation and praise for Count Annibale Gambara, begging his interest and his protection againt malevolent critics. This was the accepted formula for such a document – although Vivaldi seems all his life to have been more sensitive than most to criticism.

From now on, he would depend on powerful, rich people to accept – and pay for – his compositions that were not part of his paid work for the Pietà. There was to be a delay of four years before the publication of his next collection of work.

> "He [Vivaldi] designed solos for himself that would concentrate the impassioned attention of the listener on himself as on a beloved singer at the opera.... He glorified a personal feeling, a new lyricism, the vogue for which was as widespread as it was sudden."
>
> Marc Pincherle, a scholar of Vivaldi.

Vivaldi would have composed for occasions like this. He had to earn his living by composing on demand. Fortunately, Venice, with her love of festivals, church ceremonies and processions, was constantly demanding new music. Every important visit, in this case of a princess, required a new composition that Vivaldi would willingly supply.

Antonio Vivaldi's life story can only be pieced together from the study of surviving documents, such as letters, church records and printed publicity for musical events. No books were written about him until nearly two hundred years after his death. And no formal portraits were painted of him during his lifetime.

This was not unusual in any way; we know little of the lives of any of the Venetian creative artists – we rarely even have their portraits. It has to be set against the background of Venice. In the days of her greatness she, for all her beauty, had been a cruel place. Survival as a Republic with a vast

empire was paramount and she was held together by an iron discipline. All, from the Doge himself, as the leader, and the much feared Council of Three, were elected by the handful of aristocratic families in the Golden Book. However great and successful the generals, the painters, the musicians, they were seen only as servants of the State. Even the most powerful could not leave the city without permission and had to conform to certain rules of dress. The poor were powerless and Vivaldi's family, although not very poor, was not even at the edge of the circle of influential families. Vivaldi was regarded as a rather lowly craftsman.

Ambition and success were regarded with suspicion – as Antonio Vivaldi was to learn.

He was independent minded. Even his early published music already shows him as highly individualistic, with the solo violin, instrument or voice set against the background of other instruments or voices. Before Vivaldi, the group would all play together; there were none of the virtuoso performances that stamped Vivaldi's style from the start.

Vivaldi's independent streak would continually bring him into conflict with the powerful families of Venice, as well as the board of the Pietà.

Making a living

In those days, in Italy and across Europe, composers were not idolized or wealthy. They were regarded as composing for a living, no grander or more important than a cook or a builder who built for a living. They all, alike, simply did the job they were paid for. Luckily for Vivaldi he lived in Venice, with her love of festivity and her passion for music. For every church celebration, for every festival, for every procession, for the visit of every great noble new music was called for. And the composer, like the tailor, would be expected to provide new music or clothes for the occasion.

There was no way a composer could earn enough to live on, except by producing new music. No royalties or fees of any kind were paid if music was copied and performed on any later occasion. Composers, including Vivaldi, were forced to compose not only rapidly, but for *anyone* who wanted it and was prepared to pay.

And then there was Carnival. Carnival, when there was a ceaseless demand for the lively, gay music for which Vivaldi became famous across Europe, and why his music is now so loved.

Carnival

The coming of the eighteenth century had seen Venice turn from a certain extravagance of manner to the joyful madness of Carnival.

"... entering this town [Venice], one breathes an atmosphere of voluptuousness that is scarcely conducive to morality. Nothing is to be found there but spectacle, pleasure and frivolous diversions. In other European countries, the madness of carnival lasts but a few days; here it continues for six months of the year."

Ange Goudar, a satirist, writing in 1774.

In other countries Carnival took place just before Lent, a time in the Catholic Church for austerity, penance and fasting. Men and women had a last fling, throwing off their worries and giving themselves up to a week or two of wild indulgence before settling back to normality.

Venice, however, was in love with Carnival – and their celebration lasted for six months of the year. From the first Sunday in October until March, the Venetians enjoyed the season of masquerade.

An illusion of equality

It is no wonder that Venice loved Carnival so much, with the anonimity and freedom it afforded. It was a dream – an illusion of equality, a revolution against solemn obligations. The loss of supremacy was forgotten in flirtation, in music, in laughter.

Venice had always loved pageantry, rich clothes, beautiful, extravagant objects and display – but now for weeks on end the streets, the squares and the waterways were thronged with revellers. All identities were hidden by voluminous costumes and grotesque masks. Every man was addressed simply as *Signore Maschera*, whatever his age or rank.

The English diarist, John Evelyn, had written of Carnival – "the extravagant music and a thousand gambols" – and of the game of throwing eggs filled with scented water, or worse, at passers-by. It was madness. Bulls were hunted down alley-ways. Sideshows were set up. The great square, the *Piazza San Marco*, was raucous with performing dogs, dancing bears – even a rhinoceros, who captivated the crowd and had its portrait painted.

Gambling was a mania. There was a constant call for amusement – for new delights – for music and especially for opera. The seven opera houses were filled to capacity – with audiences who talked and ate and drank throughout the performances.

And yet, combined with the buffoonery, there was a special Venetian magic, a charm, an elegance, a fantasy – that drew men and women of wealth and leisure from all over Europe to take part. These were the days of the Grand Tour – when the young

Carnival, to Venice, meant six months of revelry in disguise. This painting captures the unreality, the abandonment to pleasure that was Carnival. Vivaldi became famous for the lively and light-spirited music he composed for this wild and carefree time.

Milords of Europe trailed around the cultural cities of Italy. For them, Venice was a place of romance and excitement....

It would not have been considered at all strange that a visiting king should wear a mask. He was simply a part of Carnival.

The masked king

On December 29, 1708, Frederick IV, King of Denmark and Norway, arrived incognito in Venice. To hide his identity, he wore a Carnival mask. On the Sunday after his arrival, King Frederick IV attended a service at the Pietà. In the concert that followed, he heard the girls sing and play under the direction of the Master who was occupying the rostrum in the absence of Gasparini. The Master was in all probability Vivaldi, who, seizing the moment, wrote a suitable dedication and presented a collection of twelve sonatas for violin and harpsichord to the monarch before he left the city.

His Majesty had been greatly impressed by the

The Venetians loved opera and gambling. Swathed in their carnival cloaks, masked and anonymous, they gathered about the card-tables. As her power dwindled, so Venice's addiction to gambling grew.

music of the Pietà and was no doubt glad to accept the dedication. Vivaldi knew his music would now be on its way to a wider European audience.

To succeed as a composer in the eighteenth century, it was vital to obtain patronage among the aristocracy and people of importance. Vivaldi, like the rest of his contemporaries, made the most of every opportunity.

By now he was deeply engaged in writing the concertos that were in the end to catch the imagination of all Europe – concertos to be played not only in the salon but in church.

Ambition

However, his position at the Pietà was not as certain as it could have been. Outside its walls was a world eager for music, and Vivaldi was very well aware of the fact. But the governors were Venetians and disliked ambition in both great and little men. And to them, Antonio Vivaldi was very little indeed.

Venice acted like a magnet, drawing rich and influential visitors on their Grand Tours from all over Europe. They came for Carnival, for the festivities, the romance, the gambling, the opera – and adventure. Identities were concealed behind masks. They often left taking a piece of music or a painting with them as a reminder of their visit – which was a boost to Vivaldi and also to Venice's finances.

They praised his work, but were uneasy. He was ambitious and independent. It is probable that they thought he should be grateful for his position, and content simply to carry out his duties at the Ospedale.

Vivaldi's appointment had been renewed in 1706, but the next year by only a very narrow margin. In 1708, he seemed secure – but one vote in 1709 sent him out of office. No one is certain where he went, or what he did – but in 1711 he was back – and in 1713, the *maestro di coro*, Francesco Gasparini, left Venice for Rome. Pietro Dall'Olio was appointed in his place but he could not cope with the extraordinary demands made upon him.

Vivaldi, that most prolific of composers, leaped at the chance to provide music whenever it was needed and in 1715 was praised by the governors for producing an amazing range of over thirty compositions, covering every aspect of church ritual – as well as teaching the girls.

Another *maestro di coro* followed the unfortunate Dall'Olio – and Vivaldi filled in the gaps between their appointments.

It is astounding that he managed to do any of this work, for he was becoming involved in the opera.

Opera

In the late sixteenth century a group of musicians in Florence had invented a new form of music – speech with a musical accompaniment. It was new – but it was monotonous.

However, soon after, the musician to the court of Mantua, Claudio Monteverdi, presented an entirely new type of music, with rich and splendid orchestration, choruses, ballet and beautiful songs. It was the beginning of true opera.

Monteverdi's popular opera was forgotten but opera, of another sort, remained and flourished – especially in Venice. Venice wanted to be astonished and amused. She demanded novelty. Composers found it increasingly difficult to keep up with the demands of the public for more operas, especially in the months of Carnival. Often they were driven

"If Vivaldi's work-rate constantly astounded his contemporaries, then it must have been so extraordinary that even a generation professionally given to fast and copious writing found it striking."

Walter Kolneder,
from "Antonio Vivaldi,
His Life and Work".

to refurbish old pieces, enlivening them by the introduction of new songs. Musical scores that survive are a mass of pasting over, crossing out and insertions.

Vivaldi's father, Giovanni, had composed a little for the opera (it was, after all, the bread and butter of many a musician) and he had acted as entrepreneur on a small scale. His son knew that opera was an excellent way to put his music before the public – and to supplement his income.

"Ottone in Villa"

Antonio Vivaldi decided to try his hand at opera outside Venice, in Vicenza. The Pietà's governors gave him a month's leave of absence in April 1713 – "for the exercise of his skill" – and he produced his first opera – *Ottone in Villa*.

The musical score for Vivaldi's piece "Molette" as he originally wrote it. The speed at which Vivaldi wrote, especially opera at which he averaged two a year for twenty-six years, was incredible.

The instruments of the sixteenth century were steadily evolving into those we know today. Even in Vivaldi's time, violin-making had reached perfection in the town of Cremona in Italy. The violins of Stradivarius (1644-1737) are still treasured by today's violinists – and would have made writing for the violin a joy.

He did not make great changes in his style of composition; Italy at that time would not have expected it. When he played the violin, his audience expected the same extraordinary, sparkling virtuosity, whether it was at a Pietà concert, as part of solemn religious service, or in an opera – they always expected to find the hallmarks of each composer in their work.

Vivaldi brought a creativity and style to his composition that was consistent throughout his life, whatever he wrote. Like the rest of his contemporaries, he occasionally borrowed from the works of another composer – but rarely. He preferred to borrow from himself, reworking a theme or an idea, to give it new life.

Ottone was well-received and from that moment Antonio Vivaldi was to write more and more for the operatic stage.

The Teatro San Angelo

Introducing his first Venetian opera, *Orlando finto pazzo*, in 1714, Vivaldi became involved in the management of the Teatro San Angelo. To keep any control over a production it was necessary for a composer to become involved in everything from ticket sales to attracting and keeping performers, and coping with their demands, their moods and their pay. Because of the anxieties such a position entailed and his continuing ill health, Vivaldi withdrew after only a year. The experience did not frighten him away from management and later he was to have many works performed there.

A priest working in the rather murky world of eighteenth century opera may seem strange to us, but many clergy of the time were involved in stage productions and non-religious music.

Following the success of *Orlando finto pazzo*,

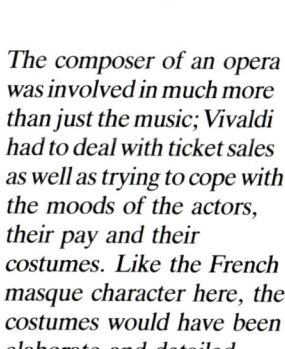

The composer of an opera was involved in much more than just the music; Vivaldi had to deal with ticket sales as well as trying to cope with the moods of the actors, their pay and their costumes. Like the French masque character here, the costumes would have been elaborate and detailed.

operas poured from Antonio Vivaldi's pen. Between 1713 and 1739, he averaged almost two a year – and this on top of all his other compositions and management work.

Chaos and drama on stage

The world of opera has always had an element of the chaotic in it. At times, in Venice, it seemed as mad as Carnival itself. The most popular singers were paid exorbitant amounts and their wishes overrode any ideas the composer might have. The number and quality of arias had to be allotted with scrupulous regard for rank. The singers preened and sulked and argued. A song that had been acclaimed in one production would have to be lifted bodily and put into another.

Wild applause at the end of an aria meant an encore – even if the character had "died" and had to scramble to their feet again. One singer insisted on appearing at the top of a stage "hill", dressed as an armed knight, whatever the opera.

The plots were melodrama at its most convoluted – mistaken identities, vendettas, betrayed brides, vengeful villains, faithful lovers. Ancient history and exotic Eastern settings were popular – palaces and grottoes and ruins.

Whatever the plot, a happy ending was essential. In one opera, *Catone in Utica*, Vivaldi was obliged to change the original, dramatic ending. In the second version, Cato, instead of committing suicide on stage as the climax, lives and capitulates to Caesar.... Tales of ancient Rome were popular, for Venice saw herself as the new Rome. Romans equated with good – barbarians with evil.

No one listened to a word of the dramatic speeches, the *recitatives*. Attention only turned to the stage from card games, food and flirtation when a popular singer launched into an aria.

The recitatives carried the plot forward. The arias froze it – and brought each scene to an end. In consequence, the plots hiccupped on to the happy finale. Miraculously, Vivaldi brought inventiveness and beauty to these creaking structures.

"Is it fanciful to discern behind the furious energy of Vivaldi's music the frustration of a man condemned from childhood to lead a sedentary life? Or to glimpse in some of the slow movements the doubts of a man outwardly so self-satisfied? This much is certain: no composer before the nineteenth century better deserves the epithet 'romantic', and no composer has written music of greater power and originality."

Michael Talbot, from *"Vivaldi"*.

A hard head for business

The business side of things was even more involved – full of dubious deals and squabbles. Vivaldi, however, had a hard business head. In one of the few descriptions we have of him he is making a brisk sale of some violin concertos – and trying to persuade the purchaser to take violin lessons from him, in order to play them properly. One gentleman was aghast that Vivaldi expected "a guinea for every piece". But cash down for a written manuscript was more lucrative and certain than income from printed works, passing through the hands of a publisher.

Venice wanted beautiful music and magnificent voices – but it also wanted spectacle. The producers were expected to provide splendid sets that amazed by their ingenuity. Mechanical animals and live horses abounded, while elaborate lighting effects and costumes made the evening one of glittering excitement.

"La Fenice"

The opera houses themselves – like the concert halls – were beautiful. Sadly, they are all gone. The one surviving opera house of the eighteenth century, *La Fenice* (the Phoenix), burned in 1836. (Such was the enthusiasm of the Venetians, the building, like the mythical Phoenix, was reborn from its ashes and reopened the very next year.)

For all the extravagance it is interesting to note that one of Vivaldi's own productions was praised as being "really nice, and very attractive to the eye; the machines were not so expensive as in the others and the orchestra not so large, but none the less it was worth hearing."

Operas were composed quickly, to answer demand, and were never expected to run for any length of time. If they had been received with great enthusiasm, they might be staged again, probably altered to a lesser or greater degree.

We know of *only* forty-five operas that Vivaldi himself composed, but when he was criticized in 1739 for "miserable" recitatives, he indignantly

In the opera of Vivaldi's day the costumes have very little to do with the period in which the plot is set. Quite clearly, not a great deal of attention is being paid to what is happening on the stage. The audience is chatting and flirting and would eat and drink, too – only breaking off for important arias. Vivaldi wrote and produced many such operas and suffered in the process!

declared that with ninety-four operas to his credit, he could refute such an accusation. So it appears many of his works have been lost.

In 1715, Antonio Vivaldi was immensely popular as a composer of opera – but far greater fame was about to find him.

The concerto

With the appearance in 1711 of his first published set of concertos, *L'estro armonico*, Europe had discovered genius. The innovations in form were striking enough, but it was the passion and energy of the music that amazed everyone who heard it.

The collection was dedicated to the Grand Prince Frederick of Tuscany – a skilled musician in his own right and patron to such notable composers as Scarlatti, Albinoni and Handel. In his dedication,

Vivaldi praised his new Dutch publisher. This man not only printed the music with far more accuracy than Vivaldi's previous publisher, but saw that it had a much wider distribution. For Vivaldi, having his composition published north of the Alps meant that all Europe could begin to know his work.

The concerto – of a sort – was already established in Italy. They usually had four movements while Vivaldi's concertos moved to three movements, as is common today. Before Vivaldi's time *groups* of instruments played against one another – a form known as *concerti grossi*. Vivaldi moved in the direction of the modern form, where a solo instrument is given prominence, but he often used several leading instruments. Musicians in Italy were slow to adjust to Vivaldi's innovations, but in northern Europe, where the form scarcely existed, Vivaldi made a great impact. His work became the inspiration for a generation of composers.

Musicians and the public élite were fascinated by his music. Vivaldi's own mastery of the violin – in the dramatic and flamboyant manner of Italy, as opposed to the more sober technique of northern Europe – caused him to compose for strings in a way that was adventurous and dazzling. The precise, edgy form of the fast movements was set against a melancholy in the slow movements that perhaps mirrored the sadness in Italy that lay beneath the gaiety of Carnival.

"... by revolutionizing the new concerto and turning what had been a fairly localized vogue for the new form into a continent-wide passion, Vivaldi actually managed to revolutionize the very language of music."
Michael Talbot, from "Vivaldi".

Vivaldi's variations

One of the innovations used by Vivaldi to bring added interest to his later concertos was the grouping of "cells" of notes, not in the accepted pairs, but in threes. With pairs, one had simply been balanced against the other. Ternary grouping allowed a far greater flexibility. Sometimes the construction of phrases was given a spiky originality by his pruning the repetitive phrase to disturb the symmetry. There was none of the old feeling of inevitability in his melodies. They seemed to gain a new vivacity – a new element of surprise.

His music was bold, original and full of experiment. As biographer Michael Talbot writes: "He

> *"Vivaldi's concertos follow the fast-slow-fast order which was the style of the time and was to remain so for many years to come, but within that order there is a wealth of invention, a dazzling display of colour and harmony. The concerto No. 10 of Opus III for four violins is one example of a concerto following the established order but exploring an intensely varied musical world. The opening allegro is powerfully engaging ... and the finale of the last movement introduces a new irrepressible energy and a brilliance of harmony that is quite breathtaking."*
>
> John Booth, from his biography, "Vivaldi".

seems to delight in teasing the listener, unexpectedly freezing the movement and then, once the ear has adjusted to the slower pace, suddenly unleasing a quickfire series of chords."

At times Vivaldi was reproached for the steady, sometimes monotonous, bass line – but over this he could lay brilliantly original inventions – often using syncopation. With an elaborately structured bass, this top line would have had to be far more restricted. Previously the concerto leaned heavily on orchestral doubling, when an instrument in the orchestra played the same notes as the soloist, therefore "doubling" the melody, and on patches of "display" by the violin or cello as part of the orchestra. With Vivaldi, the soloist gained greater prominence – no doubt because he was a violinist of imagination and superb technique. The three-movement form became predominant, although about thirty concertos revert to the four-movement cycle of the church sonata – having a slow opening movement, no doubt to add solemnity to saints days or funeral services.

Vivaldi's influence

It is not only in the violin concertos that Vivaldi excelled. His orchestra offered him every opportunity for experiment. He seems to have had a great love for the cello. From the very beginning he was writing concertos for this instrument – and with greater perception and inventiveness than any of his contemporaries. The cello sonatas, too, are very remarkable – thought by many to be the finest instrumental music Vivaldi ever wrote.

The cello has two roles – as tenor and bass – and Vivaldi often sets up a dialogue between the two voices.

He appears to write best for the deeper instruments. He composed sixteen bassoon concertos, delighting in its rich, deep tone and writing both dreamingly lyrical as well as robust, humorous passages. Vivaldi made considerable demands on his bassoon players, which shows that standards at that time must have been very high.

He was the first to develop the ideas inherent in

Above: China's first all-women chamber orchestra would surely delight in playing Vivaldi's music as it was composed for the female Pietà orchestra.
Left: The last night of the Proms, London. With radio, television and modern recording techniques, we can have the very greatest performances in our own homes. In Vivaldi's day, people had to travel great distances. However, live performances are still popular for passionate music lovers.

> "In the broadest circles of connoisseurs and amateurs Antonio Vivaldi is known only as a composer of concertos. Yet his work embraces all the musical genres, extending from sonatas for melodic instruments with figured bass to oratorios and operas."
>
> Walter Kolneder, from "Antonio Vivaldi, His Life and Work".

the work of earlier composers and then to go on to develop the true concerto. Vivaldi was undoubtedly the most influential composer in the early development of the concerto and we know of four hundred and ninety-eight of his concertos. His influence on the great world composers that followed, such as Haydn, Beethoven, and the modern Sir Michael Tippett, was profound. His ripieno concertos (string orchestras without soloists) employed fugue – and influenced the development of the classical symphony.

Vivaldi had no false modesty – but even he could not have foreseen the influence his work was to have all over the world.

An inimitable style

By 1715, when Antonio Vivaldi was forty, his music was being eagerly sought after. An influential and rich German, Von Uffenbach, introduced Vivaldi's work to a Strasburg music society. While visiting Venice, he heard Vivaldi play and invited Vivaldi to his rooms. Vivaldi dazzled Von Uffenbach with his "very difficult and quite inimitable [improvisation] on the violin", and ten *concerti grossi* were ordered in consequence. Three days later, Vivaldi arrived with the music, "which he claimed to have composed especially for me." It was on this occasion that Vivaldi then offered the purchaser music lessons – presumably to ensure his music would be played correctly – but also to make a little extra from the transaction.

It was Von Uffenbach who wrote of the extraordinary contrast between the excitement of Carnival that swept the city, and the calm, beautiful voices of the nuns and girls singing Vespers in the Ospedali. The beauty and peace of Vivaldi's religious music was enough to make him one of the world's great composers. But Vivaldi belonged to both worlds – San Marco, the Ospedale and his old home all lay within easy distance of each other.

From that square mile of the city his fame had spread across Europe. But to many, despite the success of his concertos and his religious works, Vivaldi was predominantly a composer of operas.

The frontispiece, as it would have been published at the time, of one of Vivaldi's most influential sets of music.

"Juditha triumphans"

In 1716, he was commissioned to write the Carnival opera, *La constanza trionfante degl'amori e degl'odi*. His work outside the Pietà was undermining his standing there – but he restored his reputation by composing a new religious composition for them – *Juditha triumphans*.

Vivaldi had already given them *Moyses Deus Pharaonis* in 1714, but we now only have the libretto (words). *Juditha* we still have in its entirety.

Song of triumph and hope

The libretto (words) of this sacred choral work, or oratorio, was an allegory of Venice (Judith) standing against the enemy (Holophernes). As we have seen, Venice had lost much of her ancient command of the sea and was still suffering humiliating defeat at the hands of the Turks. In 1716, the Turks began a siege of Corfu, a Venetian strong-hold – but Venice continued to hope that the series of disasters she had endured could be halted.

By the time *Juditha* was performed, the Turkish commander had been killed and the siege abandoned. The oratorio was given as a song of triumph and hope.

There had been a tradition of these religious oratorios at the Pietà long before Vivaldi's time. The subjects were usually to do with celebrated Biblical heroines, as the cast was entirely female. We know that the young ladies coped with the male parts – we come across "Paulina dal Tenor" and "Anneta dal Basso". The accompanying instrumentation added depth and strength to the "male" roles.

In writing the oratorio, Vivaldi made full use of the Pietà's collection of instruments – some were so outlandish as to invite mockery from critics. The score of *Juditha* calls for two recorders, two oboes, soprano chalumeau, two clarinets, two trumpets with timpani, mandolin, four theorboes, obbligato organ, five viola all'inglese and viola d'amore, as well as strings and continuo.

Instruments at this time were evolving rapidly and many were used very differently than today.

> "... Vivaldi's strength lies far more in the unmistakable personality which he stamps on all his compositions in every genre – a factor which redeems many an otherwise undistinguished work. No doubt he became aware of his own idiosyncrasies early on and like many other great composers paraded them a little too glibly at times. But without these 'vivaldisms' his music would lack its peculiar sense of urgency, of drama, of pathos, of buoyancy – qualities which his contemporaries and successors could not recapture even as they tried to model themselves on him."
>
> Michael Talbot, from "Vivaldi".

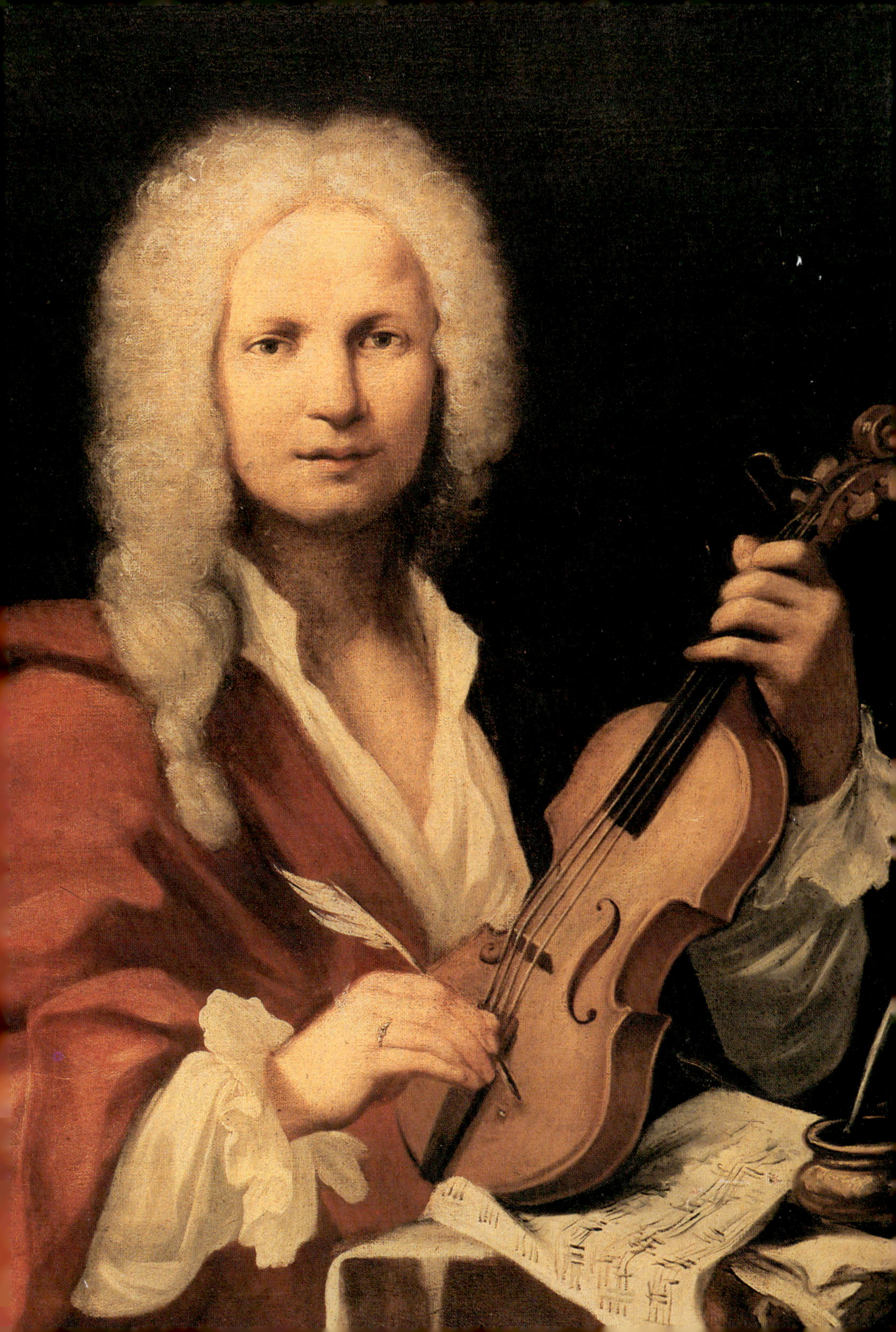

Vivaldi, always full of experiments and original ideas, probably enjoyed every new instrument. It may also have been that the Pietà used such a wide range of instruments to attract the crowds to their concerts.

The trumpet, used extensively in *Juditha,* was very important not only to Vivaldi, but to Venice. It was one of the symbols of her power and played a great part in the ceremonial that celebrated her glory. In some of the concertos, the violin is used as *violino in trombe* (violin imitating a trumpet) to bring brilliance to a passage.

Characterization

Despite his awkwardness with librettos, Vivaldi could combine words, however weak, with musical comment to create most moving passages. In both oratorio and opera, he could illuminate the action with instrumental effects. In opera, however extreme the plot, Vivaldi had the ability to wrench the heart. The emotions of a bewildered, angry woman are echoed by the accompaniment. When she is on the edge of collapse, the music swoons with her. Her lover fears that she is dead, and the violins describe his horror in descending chords as they fall.

In oratorio, too, he could paint the clash of arms, a swallow's flight to its nest, the whinnying of a war horse, the voice of its rider, the buffeting of the wind – though there was far more to his music than such effects.

Antonio Vivaldi had his faults. On occasions an image that has been astoundingly apt at one point, recurs when the moment has passed – musical need ousting dramatic sense.

Having no male voices in the Pietà, Vivaldi was obliged to give the masculine roles strength and depth by the use of the supporting instruments.

There are no duets in the oratorio, just as there are few duets in the operas of the period. A chorus, doubling as Assyrian warriors and Bethulian maidens as required, was used to carry forward the plot, interjecting the solo arias with comment.

Above: Many of the musical instruments of Vivaldi's period were only just evolving into those we recognize today – but the violin had already reached perfection. Each violin-maker created a different "voice" in his instrument. Sadly, many violins are now bought not to be played, but as instruments to be locked away to gain in value. The great composers of the past knew their compositions would be played on instruments worthy of their dreams.

Opposite: A portrait of Vivaldi painted in 1723, when he was forty-five. It is probably greatly idealized, as portraits were at that time.

> "Vivaldi's ability as a word-painter is unrivalled for his period. It is remarkable how pictorial significance can permeate the whole of the texture, bringing simple accompanimental figures into relief. The obsessional quality of Vivaldi's natural musical thought, which can, in extreme cases, sustain a single idea for the duration of the entire movement, helps to establish a basic 'affection' for the movement...."
>
> Michael Talbot, from his biography, "Vivaldi".

> "At a time when the printing of music and the distribution of printed music were in their infancy, and consequently the resident 'maestro di cappella' had to satisfy the enormous demand for music largely from his own pen, rapid production was almost a professional precondition for a bandmaster and was quite common among the composer's contemporaries."
>
> Walter Kolneder, from "Antonio Vivaldi, His Life and Work".

The actual characterization falls to the orchestra rather than the soloists – Judith having the "feminine" backing of viola d'amore and mandolin. Vagaus, the henchman of Holophernes, flatters him with oboe and recorder. Holophernes has orchestral strings to support "his" manly arias, although in wooing Judith "he" is given the caressing notes of oboe and obbligato organ.

With the background of the rambling, rather shapeless operas of the period, the oratorio also suffers from weakness of plotting. However, the music for the moment when Vagaus discovers the beheaded Holophernes and is overcome by horror and anger, is overwhelming.

Mantua

In 1716, Antonio Vivaldi's operas once more began to appear at San Angelo and others followed.

With the drama and beauty of *Juditha triumphans,* Vivaldi had once again earned the Pietà's approval, but he was not reappointed to the Pietà in 1718. He had gone to the small city state of Mantua.

Italy of the eighteenth century was a collection of such small states – unification into one country scarcely a dream. It was, as it is today, a place for tourists – but tourists prepared to endure bad roads, worse inns, even brigans in the south. Artists and musicians, however, moved constantly from city to city in search of employment and patronage.

Mantua had a long history of patronage – and the support of the arts continued under the rule of Prince Philip. It was to Mantua that Vivaldi went to take up a post as director of music at the court.

His duties were mainly to compose non-religious works but he was given the opportunity to write for many different occasions – including a cantata for the installation of a bishop and another in praise of the Prince. During his stay he wrote several operas and reworked old librettos.

The handwritten score of the work, *Tito Manlio,* was inscribed: *Musico del Vivaldi, fatta in 5 giorni* – music written by Vivaldi in five days. It is astounding that a man with poor health should be capable of producing such quantities of work and at such speed – his manuscripts often start off neatly written, but soon his eagerness to get his ideas onto paper reduce the notes to a scrawl. He was able to write his scores even more quickly than a professional copyist could reproduce them! Perhaps it was the very fact that Antonio Vivaldi's health prevented his other activities that all his energies were directed into his music.

Most of his solo cantatas were written in Mantua. Singers under the patronage of great men were lent by them to sing at various performances during the opera season. Once it was over they all came home to roost. They were expected to entertain the court and visitors and Vivaldi's *tours de force* gave them the opportunity to show the range and brilliance of their voices. He felt very confident and was at the height of his career – and at the height of his fame across Europe.

It was perhaps in Mantua that Vivaldi met Anna Giraud – known as La Girò or Annina della Pietà, a lady who had a good voice but even greater acting ability. She was often to perform in Vivaldi's operas and she and her sister, Paolina, would accompany him on his travels for the rest of his life. As he was a priest, and therefore celibate, gossip followed them. Vivaldi denied, with great indignation, that there was any impropriety in their friendship.

Vivaldi, aged forty-three, eventually left Mantua in 1721, but his work continued to be performed there after he had left.

This was the book by Benedetto Marcello that laughed at the practices of Venetian musicians – and especially Vivaldi. Marcello was from the upper classes and in such a class-conscious society must have been aggravated by the fame of this barber's son. Marcello and Vivaldi probably never met. Vivaldi is the small angel wearing a priest's hat, who fiddles as he steers the boat.

"Il teatro alla moda"

In December 1720 a book appeared – *Il teatro alla moda* – The Theatre In Fashion – by Benedetto Marcello. It was to shatter much of Antonio Vivaldi's confidence and damage his reputation. It was a satire that mocked a great many of the people connected, directly or indirectly, with opera in Venice, and most particularly Vivaldi.

The illustration on the title page shows a rather odd group of characters in a boat with Vivaldi as an angel in a priest's hat, playing the violin, one

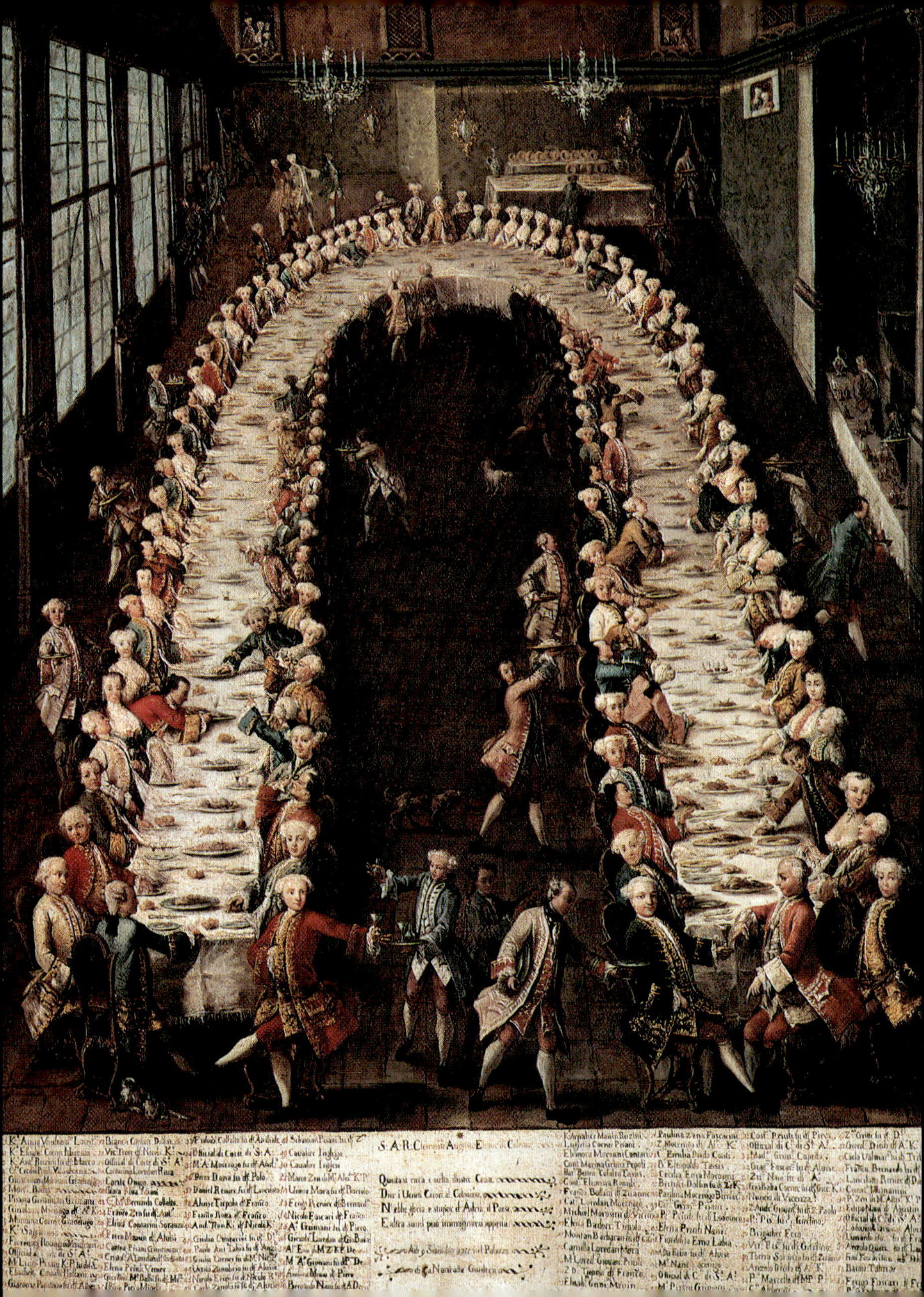

foot on the rudder, the other beating time, depicting him as both opera manager and musician. The book held up to ridicule all Vivaldi's musical weaknesses – the lengthy cadenzas, the muting of which he was so fond, the use of outlandish instruments. It mocked his dedications with their abject humility. It sneered at his shaky skills as a librettist. It was very cruel – and there was enough truth in it to make it bite hard.

Three years before, Vivaldi's father had been involved in a scandal over debt and mismanagement at the *Teatro San Angelo*. Vivaldi himself had worked there frequently as conductor and impresario. Marcello's family partly owned the site and there had been long legal battles – on top of which Marcello was one of the accepted inner circle of Venetian society, a noble of a leading family.

He must have resented this priest who wrote, not as a gifted amateur, but for money – a man whose father was a mere barber. In truth, even while Venice loved Vivaldi's music, they despised him. Rank mattered in the Serene Republic.

The book affected Vivaldi's career in Venice badly. None of his operas appeared on the Venetian stage for three years after it was published.

Fame and recognition

If Venice had turned its back on him, the rest of the Italian states were eager for his operas. It is hard to follow him as he travels to and fro between cities and opera houses. He seems to have been in Milan in 1721, in Rome in 1723 and again in 1724 at Carnival. He was immensely proud of the fact that twice the Pope invited him to his private apartments to play. He was moving in distinguished circles – in particular that of Cardinal Pietro Ottoboni. We have a caricature of Vivaldi made at this time – beak-nosed and vividly alive. Rome loved both his music and his virtuosity as a violinist and his visit was a triumph.

The Pietà had not forgotten him, despite his absence, nor he the Pietà. He supplied them with two concertos, for the annual church celebration, the Feast of the Visitation ... something that their

Above: An even more idealized portrait of Vivaldi. Here he is holding an unfinished score with the pen and ink lying ready.

Opposite: Vivaldi moved among the wealthiest Italian circles. He had to – they were his employers. As a composer, Vivaldi simply provided a service when asked to do so – just like a servant did. As a result, he was entirely dependent upon the patronage of nobles and the great variety of his music reflects the wide range of sources of his income.

Unlike the paintings of Vivaldi this lively caricature gives us a good idea of Vivaldi's nature. In all caricatures the most prominent feature is made more of – here it is quite clearly Vivaldi's nose!

"What strikes me most about 'The Four Seasons' is how Vivaldi evokes such strong images in such a direct way. The fast passages bristle with energy, the melodies communicate with beauty and simplicity; and the huge contrasts in the music enhance the effect of this on the listener."

Nigel Kennedy,
a famous violinist.

otherwise worthy staff were unable to do. The governors decided to ask him to write two concertos for them every month and they paid him a suitable fee. If he was in Venice he would be required to direct rehearsals. If absent, he could send the music. Just as long as he paid the postage.

Gone was their old attitude of condescension to an employee. Vivaldi was too famous and too great now. It was an arrangement agreed between equals.

In December 1725 a new collection of Vivaldi's music was advertised in the Amsterdam Gazette – twelve concertos entitled *Il cimento dell'armoni e dell inventione* (the contest between harmony and invention). The opening four works were called *Le quattro stagione* – The Four Seasons.

"The Four Seasons"

Vivaldi lived two hundred and fifty years ago. He wrote for a society that we can scarcely imagine. His output was prolific – yet one composition more than any other he wrote has spoken to our time, and for many has been the door to classical music.

In the music of earlier times, if Nature was portrayed it was seen as an unimportant part of creation. In Vivaldi it is Nature herself that is dominant. In the eighteenth century, Europe "discovered" Nature. However sophisticated a lifestyle, it was becoming fashionable to sigh for the simple life of the countryside, although romanticism did not reach its height until the end of the century. The nobility of Venice, that uniquely confined city, retreated to their country villas when Carnival was over and the heat became unbearable – to live very much the life they lived in town. Until Carnival came around again.

When Vivaldi wrote "The Four Seasons", he was conjuring up the dream world of peasantry and nature. He wrote four sonnets to describe the seasons of the year and the score is most carefully marked to show exactly what each musical passage describes.

In *La Primavera* (The Spring) three violins "sing" as a chorus of birds – and soften to the murmuring of a little breeze. Rippling, quick notes describe a running brook. In one section, the viola is marked *Il cane che grida* – the barking dog – and in another a solo violin, *Capraro che darme*, describes a sleeping goatherd.

Thunder and lightning of a sudden storm are evoked by the agitation of the violins and rapidly rising scales. The storm past, the music calms once more and the birds take up their song again, chirruping in the sunlight.

L'estate (Summer) is a time of burning heat and the drone of flies. It is in this section that Vivaldi brings in two birds that are to make a reappearance in later works – the goldfinch and the cuckoo.

L'autunno (Autumn/Fall) is, in Italy, the time of the wine harvest and hunting. This is no picture of a golden-leaved landscape, but of tipsy shepherds trying to dance, and of the chase. Vivaldi himself links the written description of the drunken peasants dancing and then falling asleep, followed by an early morning hunt, to the music. He adds comments on what is to be expressed.

The piece begins with a peasant tune – then, in a passage marked *L'Ubriaco* (The Drunkard), broken chords lurching over nearly three octaves bring the drunken crew, at last, to wine-heavy sleep.

Anyone who has experienced Venice in winter – the cutting winds scouring the deserted squares and whipping the Lagoon – will understand *L'inverno* (Winter).

Vivaldi paints it clearly – the crackle of ice, the raw air – and the world indoors. With the lower strings he summons up a picture of home and firelight – while the upper violins imitate the rain spattering against the windows.

It was the first time Vivaldi had used music to give exact descriptions – and many composers were to be inspired by it. So great was the impact of the concertos that a tradition of this type of music began that led on to Haydn's "The Seasons" and Beethoven's "Pastoral Symphony".

The music enchanted the eighteenth century as much as it has our own. The French especially delighted in it. In 1730, the King of France had a

> *"Vivaldi is one of those rare composers whose work cuts across the usual divisions of classical and 'other' music. His music has a freshness and vitality which reaches 20th-century listeners as effortlessly as it did those of the 18th century when the music was first heard. Perhaps this appeal can be explained by the sense of a powerful human presence in his work, an irrepressible, energetic personality."*
>
> John Booth, from his biography, "Vivaldi".

> *"If the performer does not make the listener aware that in Vivaldi a scale or a broken chord can represent a man's inner disturbance (L'Inquietudine!) caused by his fear of ghosts (Fantasmi!) and of natural forces (Tempesta!), he himself cannot have felt the forces from which Vivaldi's notes arose."*
>
> Walter Kolneder, from "Antonio Vivaldi, His Life and Work".

The lavish concerts given in France were wonderful occasions for Vivaldi to compose for. He wrote several operas for the French court and they would have been presented with extravagance such as this. "La sera festeggiante" is thought to have been performed at the Palace of Versailles.

sudden desire to hear *La primavera* (The Spring) yet again and an impromptu orchestra had to be put together ... several noblemen being pressed into service to supplement the professionals.

Vivaldi wrote three short operas for the French court at about this time. It may well be that they were performed in that most dazzling of palaces, Versailles – and listened to by the bewigged and painted, exquisitely gowned and utterly useless courtiers who inhabited that strange world.

Out of fashion

Time had healed, to some extent, the harm done by the book, *Il Teatro alla Moda,* and during the Carnival seasons of 1726, 1727, and 1728, Vivaldi was once more at the San Angelo as *direttore delle opere* (Director of Opera). However, he also seems to have been in Naples during this period and to have put on two new operas in Florence; one in 1727, the other in 1729.

One eminent Venetian reported in 1727, when Antonio Vivaldi was nearly fifty years old, that he had composed three operas in less than three months – "two for Venice, and the third for Florence; the last has re-established the theatre of that city and brought in much money."

Vivaldi's skills were as great, his popularity high – and yet a small chill was in the air. Venice was growing bored with Vivaldi and his contemporaries in the Venetian musical world. She had discovered the Neapolitans, who wrote in a new style.

Vivaldi's works continued to be performed, but usually in the less important places. They were no longer fashionable. The great days in Venice were coming to an end.

But there were other cities. Vivaldi now concentrated on productions outside Venice.

It is hard to reconcile Vivaldi's poor health with his constant travel and musical output. He was now unable to walk but for all that, he undertook the hard journeys from city to city, proud of his friendships with the great, always eager for new projects, still able to earn a good living and, above all, still able to compose across an amazing range of music forms and emotions. From this period, passionate music, gentle holy music and happy music to set one dancing, were still being created at a furious pace.

It is not easy to keep track of Antonio Vivaldi during this period of his life. Unlike later composers, whose every movement seems to have been recorded by colleagues and admirers, Vivaldi's life is often known to us only as a series of dates, cities and compositions – pieced together after years of research by musicologists.

The singer, Anna Giraud and her sister, Paolina, were as always with him on his travels, helping him in his bouts of illness. As an entrepreneur Vivaldi put on new operas and resurrected old ones. As a composer, he continued to astound with the range of his work, the beauty and vitality of every new composition and the speed with which he wrote.

In 1729 alone, he published five concertos for violin and one without a solo instrument. And still he wrote operas....

Between 1725 and 1735 eleven of Vivaldi's operas were performed in Venice. He often returned from his travels for these productions and was back again in 1734 for the first performance of one of his greatest operas, *L'Olimpiade,* at San Angelo.

Goldoni

It was in Venice in 1735, when Vivaldi was fifty-seven, that the playwright, Goldoni, whom the city was to take to her heart, called on him. Vivaldi was wrestling with a libretto – Zeno's "Griselda", and Goldoni offered to take a look at it. At first, Vivaldi seems to have been very suspicious of the young man's ability but, from Goldoni's own account, when Vivaldi saw how well the young man tackled the problems he was both grateful and enthusiastic, calling Anna Giraud and her sister to share his delight.

Goldoni tells how Vivaldi embraced and congratulated him and how he became his friend – and "never forsook me". The critics and gossips of his day can leave us with the picture of a work-obsessed, touchy, money-minded priest of doubtful morality, but in his friendships we see a quite different Vivaldi – warm-hearted and well-liked.

Back to the Pietà

In 1735, Vivaldi was once more engaged as *Maestro de Concerti* at the Pietà – and for exactly the same salary he was getting in 1704. Life had come full circle. The respect he had been shown in 1723 had evaporated. Apparently, the governors were satisfied that his wandering days were over and he settled to his old work of teaching, composing and conducting rehearsals. But not for long....

We have a correspondence between Vivaldi and the Marquis Guido Bentivoglio d'Aragona that shows something of Vivaldi's life at this time – from October 1736 to January 1739. It seems to show a man fighting to keep a position that is slipping away from him. There are in it elements of bluster, vanity, pique and self-pity – and of the old wheeling and dealing. But remembering the great days, we cannot blame him.

Vivaldi, it appears from the letters, is attempting to organize an operatic season in Ferrara and is deep in the complexities of finding backing, gathering singers and writing music. He is trying to do deals over the operas to be performed – and over a totally different project at San Cassiano, which prevents him going to Ferrara to sort the matter out. Contracts, rehearsals, clashes with singers, alterations to scores, opening nights: for all his

"It is as if Vivaldi sought in church music a dignity and serenity for which his life as virtuoso and entrepreneur, invalid and globe-trotter, left him too little time."

Michael Talbot, from his biography, "Vivaldi".

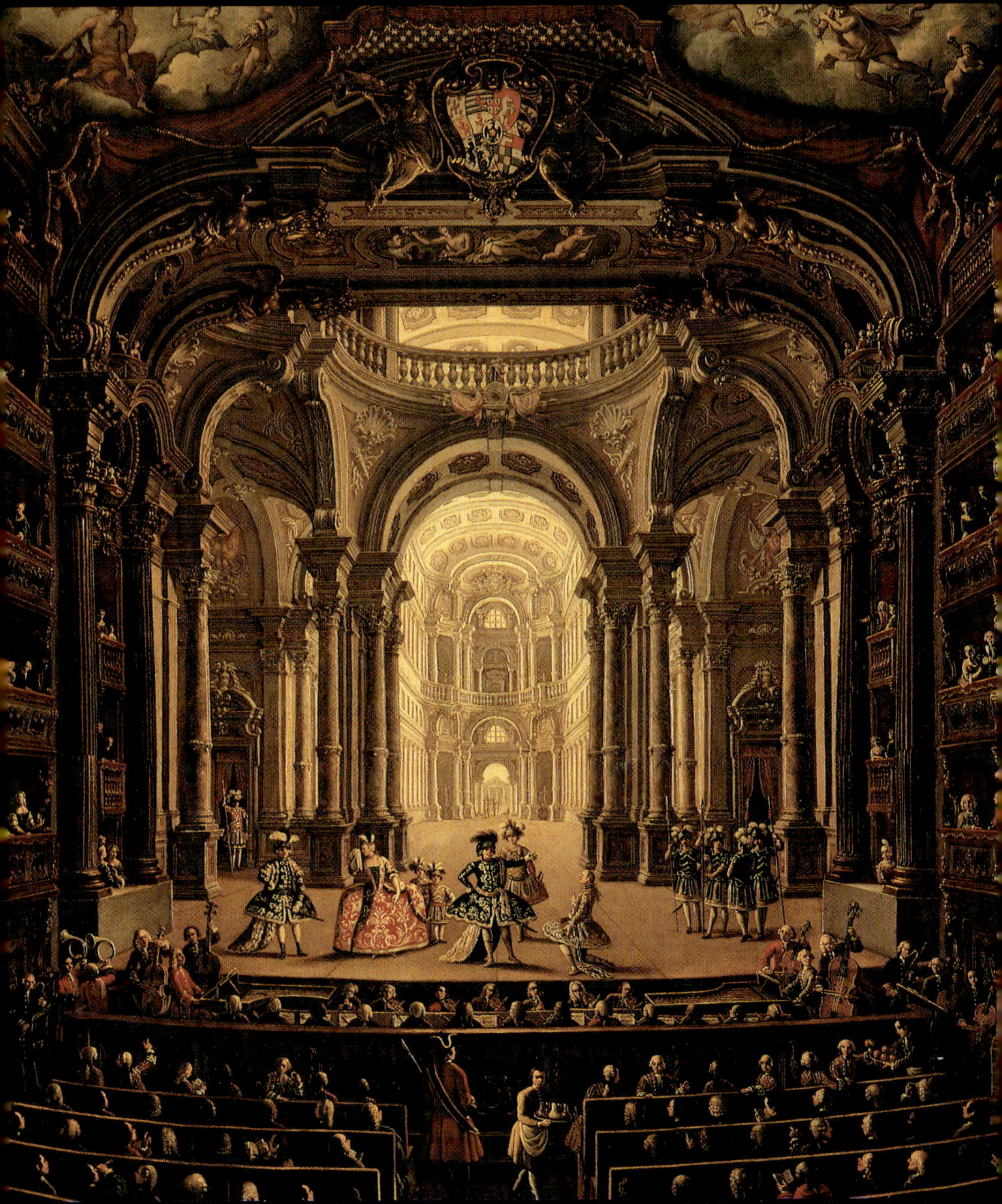

renewed association with the Pietà, he is still organizing and managing the opera. And trying to wheedle a commission for pieces for the mandolin from the worthy Marquis – who does not rise to the bait.

There is a good deal of argument with representatives of the Ferrara patrons – and chaos brought about by them constantly changing their minds. He cuts, rewrites, totally alters an original score ... and is owed money. He is very much put out when some of his work is rejected for that of another composer.

The Marquis seems more than exasperated by Vivaldi's complaints – but Vivaldi presses on with his plans. Vivaldi writes from Verona that his new opera, *Catone in Utica,* has had a great success – and that one like it would go down very well in Ferrara. Can he meet the Marquis in Ferrara to discuss matters? The Marquis says he is delighted by the news, but will not be in Ferrara that season....

There is trouble with a dancer. She has eloped with another dancer, which will play havoc with rehearsals.

Despair

Things begin to look more hopeful, but on November 16, 1737, Vivaldi is in despair. The Cardinal of Ferrara has forbidden him to enter the city – opera or no opera. This churchman was known to be very strict, and in 1738 forbade all clergy under his jurisdiction to have anything whatever to do with Carnival.

He obviously regarded Vivaldi as a blot on the priesthood – a priest who did not take church services, and who was having some sort of liaison with the opera singer, Anna Giraud.

The letters show us Vivaldi beside himself. A great deal of money is tied up in the Ferrara venture – and how can he put on an opera without Anna or trust anyone to handle the production but himself? He writes giving the reasons why he does not take services and why he needs companions to help on his travels – he is a sick man. "My travels have always been very costly because I have always had to make them with four or five persons to assist

Opposite: The "Teatro Regio" in Turin. Much of the stage architecture was illusion, created by painters and carpenters. The costumes were wildly extravagant. The audiences loved spectacle and surprise. Notice that food and drink were taken around the audience and that many people looked away from the stage to talk to their friends. At times, it must have been very disheartening for performers, musicians and producers, but it was the accepted manner. One went to see and be seen.

Above: The Doges Palace today. The Doges lived in great grandeur – using these huge rooms to receive people from all over the world. The Council of Ten (usually about thirty in number) was at the middle of a web of spies, informers and assassins and had its own rooms and prison. Stairs went down to the Bridge of Sighs over which criminals went to prison. Right: The beautiful gondolas survive, but not in their old numbers. Venice itself is being eaten away by pollution and is sinking slowly into the sea.

me." His integrity is unimpeachable – "I ... correspond with nine high princes and my letters travel all over Europe."

It must have been galling to be thwarted in all his plans by a Cardinal, when he had once been on familiar terms with such men – and with the Pope himself, and the rulers of kingdoms.

The only way to save his pocket is to have the opera, rather than himself and Anna Giraud, prohibited. That way he will at least be released from his contracts. It cannot be done – so Vivaldi is driven to hand over production to someone else – a local man acceptable to the Cardinal.

Now comes news that one of his operas, *Siroe, re di Persia,* has failed badly in Ferrara. His recitatives have been condemned as "miserable". Vivaldi is up in arms. These same recitatives have been totally successful elsewhere – it must be the fault

This scene has scarcely changed at all since Vivaldi's day – except the speed limit sign! You can imagine him hurrying to a rehearsal across the bridge. Water has always been both Venice's life and its danger. Even when Venice was going into decline, the rulers of the city spent an enormous sum to divert a river and save the city from destruction.

> "The far-reaching effect of his works, being printed in Amsterdam, Paris and London, the cultivation of his music in the most important cities of Italy and abroad, the numerous proofs of the highest recognition, all these things instilled in Vivaldi a great degree of self-esteem, all the more so since he had sprung from modest circumstances and owed his success simply and solely to intensive work centred around the Ospedale."
>
> Walter Kolneder, from "Antonio Vivaldi, His Life and Work".

of the appalling harpsichord player, together with the organizer, who obviously does not know what he is doing. He, Vivaldi, should be there. The Marquis is determined to keep well out of the entire affair. The whole Ferrara project has been a disaster.

Venice, for the last time

The royalty of Europe still admired Antonio Vivaldi's work and appear not to have been bothered by his morality. In December 1739, Prince Frederick Christian, the King of Poland and Elector of Saxony, came back to Venice. For one last time Vivaldi returned to the Pietà – his nest of singing birds – to take part in a splendid concert.

Venice loved royal visits. It was so good an excuse to arrange lavish entertainments. The city was *en fête*, with bullfights, feasting, jousting and music. Three of the Ospedali gave concerts for Frederick.

On March 21, the Pietà gave a serenata – *Il coro delle muse* – for which Vivaldi wrote a sinfonia and three concertos. He was doing what he loved best – writing for unusual combinations of instruments and with all the old imagination and attack. One concerto was written for two violins, two recorders, two trumpets, two mandolins, two salmoe, two theorbos and cello – with string orchestra and basso continuo – the same sort of eccentric instrumentation that had so annoyed Vivaldi's critics – but had given such pleasure to his admirers.

It is good to think of that spring evening – the canals illuminated, the gondolas setting down their wonderfully-dressed passengers at the doors of the Pietà, the glorious music drifting out on the night air. For a moment, time seemed to have turned back.

It was Vivaldi's last, bright farewell to Venice. It seems now that he had decided to leave Italy and settle in Austria. No doubt he hoped for the friendship and patronage of the Emperor, Charles VI, and a safe haven.

But in October 1740, Charles VI died. There was to be no patronage, no talk of music, no serenity in old age.

The last days

Antonio Vivaldi was out of fashion. He was old and he was ill. The weakness that had haunted him all his life had caught him at last. Charles de Brosses wrote of him "He is a vecchio [old man] who composes furiously and prodigiously."

Perhaps he could have gone to Dresden, where he had friends. Perhaps he could have gone to Count Morzin in Bohemia. But, at the end of July 1741, Antonio Vivaldi, aged sixty-three, died in Vienna.

We know nothing of the circumstances of his death save those in the records of the church of St. Stephen, which reported that he had died of an internal inflammation.

He was buried in the Hospital Burial Ground. The house where he died has gone, and the burial ground has vanished under a road.

His funeral was simple, but the poverty of the ceremony should not be exaggerated.

Certainly, he was not buried with great ceremony, but there was a small peal of bells, six pallbearers, six choir boys. It seems enough for a man who, despite his involvement in the gaudy world of opera, had written religious music of most unbelievable beauty.

The funeral cost nineteen florins and forty-five kreutzers, as against the hundred florins that would have been spent on the burial of a nobleman. But the gulf between the nobility and a secular priest, of whatever gifts, was very great.

Perhaps his constant friend, Anna Giraud, and her sister, Paolina, were there. We do not know. Vivaldi had slipped away into obscurity – and, on that summer day in 1741, it seemed he was utterly forgotten.

Revival

Vivaldi was dead – and in Italy it was as if his music had died with him, Venice had found other amusements – for, after all, music was ephemeral, to be enjoyed and then forgotten for something new. As always, new compositions were demanded for all occasions – and the most brilliant works were left behind.

"As opposed to listeners of today, who will accept music written within a period of at least 300 or 400 years, Vivaldi's listeners were entirely geared to 'first performances'. That Bach wrote several complete yearly cycles of cantatas because his public wanted to hear 'new music' every Sunday and Feast Day is a reflection of a situation that would be quite unthinkable today."

Walter Kolneder,
from "Antonio Vivaldi,
His Life and Work".

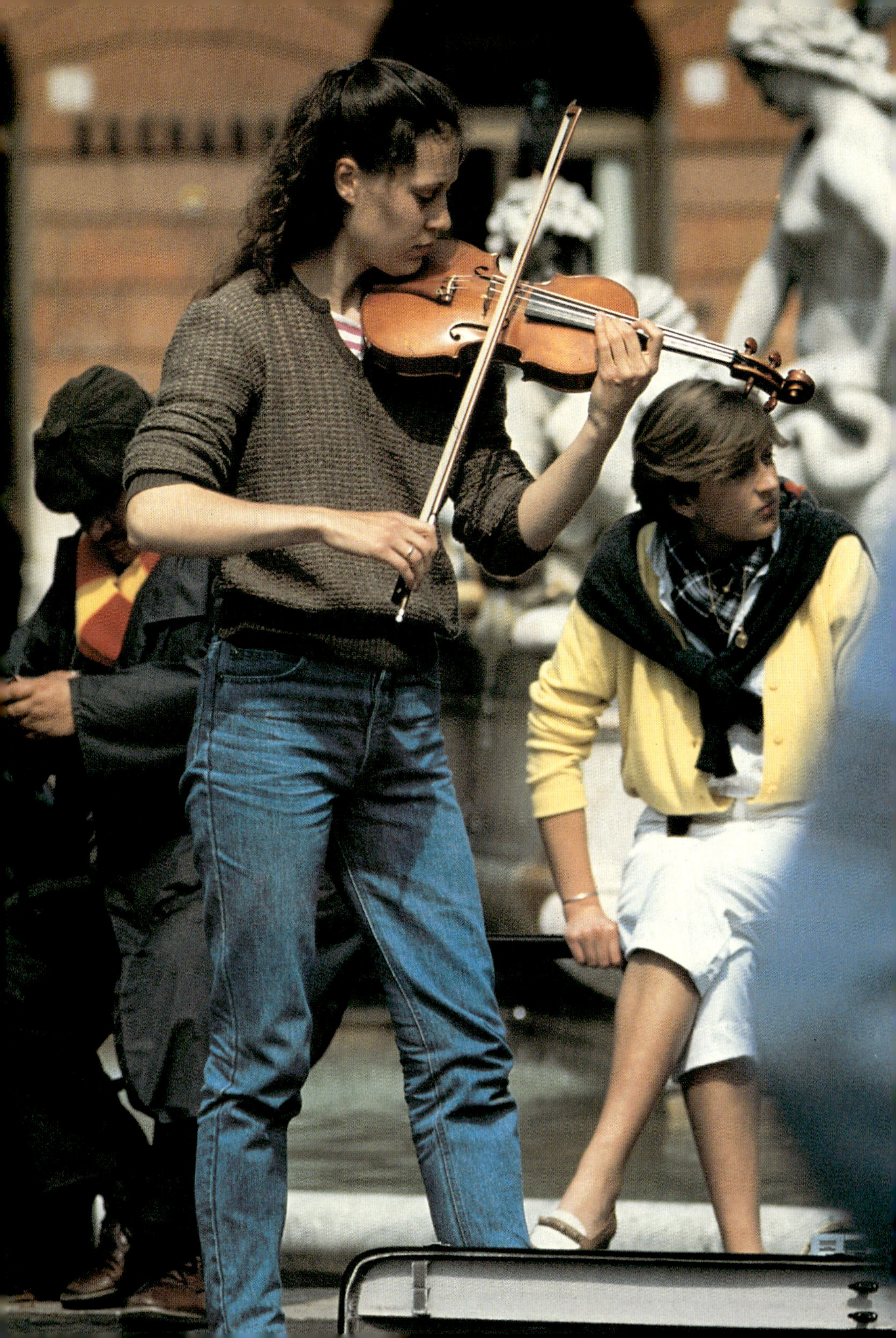

Above: Vivaldi's church music shows an entirely different side to his nature. It is in his religious music that Vivaldi shows his ability to express a deep spirituality. Vivaldi's music is played as often today in the street setting as in the church.

If he was still referred to by scholars, it was usually with contempt, although occasionally they allowed individual compositions merit. Of one concerto, Professor William Hayes of Great Britain wrote: "The principal subjects [melodies] are well-invented, well-maintained, the whole properly diversified with masterly contrivances, and the harmony full and complete" although he feels, "he had too much mercury in his constitution" and gave himself over to "a certain brilliance of fancy and execution." In other words – lacking in solid worth.

But whatever was said, no one played his music any more.

It was not until the world began to realize the genius of Johann Sebastian Bach that Vivaldi's name began to attract notice again.

A scholar gained very valuable information from Bach's eldest sons regarding Vivaldi's influence on him. Apparently, Bach had, when young, found it hard to discipline his compositions. He was, as he was later in life to describe other beginners, a "hussar of the keyboard".

Having seen some of Vivaldi's published violin

Opposite: Vivaldi's music is still alive today, being played by street musicians in Rome, London, Paris and New York. His compositions are more accessible and are being enjoyed by millions of people all over the world.

55

> *"Vivaldi's musical output was prodigious, even in an age of prolific composers. More than 800 works have been authenticated: sonatas, sinfonias, concertos, operas, cantatas and oratorios. His contribution to the concerto form was considerable; he composed more than 450 and his composition of operatic work was on the same giant scale. He composed more than 48 and claimed to have composed twice that number. Such industry is breathtaking as is the breadth of the musical language employed."*
>
> John Booth, from his biography, "Vivaldi".

concertos, Bach was very impressed and arranged several of them for the clavier. "He studied the progression of the ideas and their relationships, variety in modulation and many other things."

At first, musicologists were intrigued, but felt it was Bach's genius alone that had transformed Vivaldi's compositions. These German critics heard Vivaldi with ears accustomed to the German style of writing and believed he was merely a violinist who had composed a little, a man of small imagination or depth, making up for his deficiencies with superficialities, as a violinist embroiders a basic melody.

Then, in 1905, came Arnold Schering's history of the concerto and his statement that: "instrumentation revealed Vivaldi to be as exemplary for the shaping of the concerto as Corelli was for that of the sonata."

Interest in his work was reviving. The great and flamboyant violin virtuoso, Fritz Kreisler, took to composing in the style of Vivaldi – and the violinist and musicologist, Marc Pincherle, became inspired to dedicate his life to researching the composer.

Lost ...

In 1922, a complete list of Vivaldi's known work was published – and that seemed to be that.

The aggravating fact remained that he was known to have been a most prolific composer – a matter of some scorn to a generation of musicians which did not have to write fast, and to demand, in order to earn a living. Operas, concertos, religious compositions – where was the rest of his music?

It was known that Turin had, like Mantua, been an artistic city in the eighteenth century – and that when the entire court had fled to Sardinia to escape Napoleon's advance into Italy, the music of the court orchestra had been left behind. When they returned, it had vanished.

A professor of music at Turin University, Alberto Gentili, knew that it was believed to be held in a monastery. This story proved to be correct – the music was in the hands of the monks at the Collegio

San Carlo in Monferrato. In 1926 they asked the Turin National Library to value their vast collection, as the money was needed to carry out repairs to the monastery. The monks had been given the collection by a Genoese nobleman who had been Austrian ambassador to Venice soon after Vivaldi's death. There were ninety-five volumes of music – fourteen by Vivaldi. The library certainly could not afford to buy them, but a gentleman, Robert Foa, agreed to fund the enterprise, in memory of his little boy, Mauro, who had recently died.

... and found

It was found there were in the collection one hundred and forty instrumental works by Vivaldi, twenty-nine cantatas, twelve operas and an oratorio. Satisfaction, however, led to further frustration. It was obvious from the numbering of the pieces that a great many more existed and were still missing. The search resumed.

The descendant of the donor, Durazzo, was found – a cantankerous old man who was furious that the monks had sold his family's bequest. It was only with the help of his priest that he was at last wheedled into letting Gentili into his library. And there they were – the missing manuscripts.

Three years went by and still the old nobleman held doggedly to his collection. When he did agree to sell, the price was again completely beyond the library's funds. But another Turin patron was found – Filippo Giordano, who had, by a tragic coincidence, also lost his little son, Renzo. In his name the manuscripts were purchased and the combined collection entitled the "Collezione Mauro Foa e Renzo Giordano".

The Marchese remained awkward to the end. It took a court case to get permission for the works to be published and performed.

In 1939, as World War II was about to erupt in Europe, a festival of music taken from the Vivaldi collection was presented in Siena, Italy.

Vivaldi's music had risen from two hundred years of obscurity.

"The enthusiasm for Vivaldi and baroque music shows no sign of diminishing. Indeed, interest in the period is increasing: public demand for this kind of music is shown in the catalogues of the record companies as well as in the programmes of radio stations and the works of large and small orchestras."

John Booth, from his biography, "Vivaldi".

57

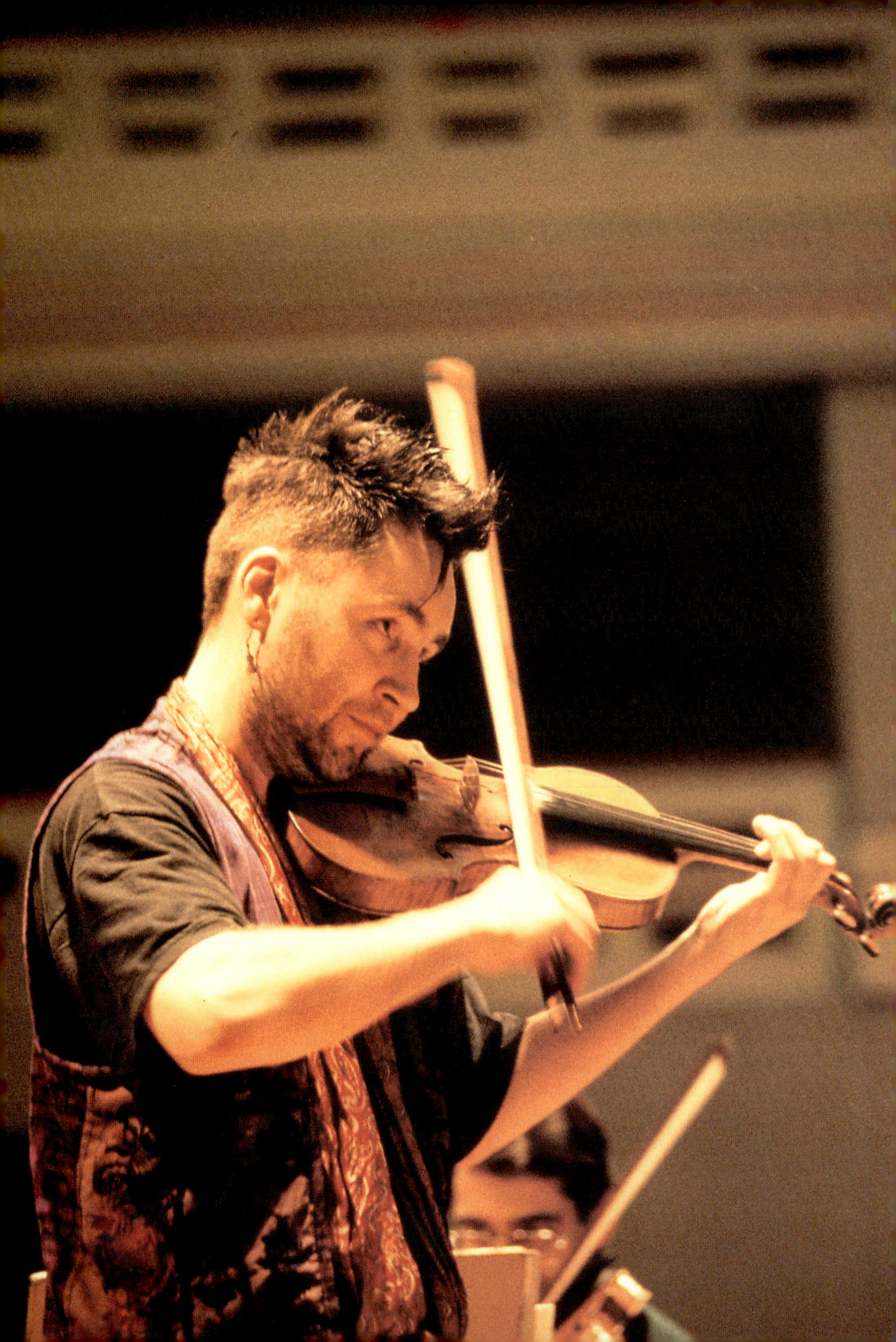

Vivaldi's legacy

At last, the twentieth century could see what the composer had achieved – and more than was widely known when he was alive. None of his cello compositions, concertos or sonatas had been published in his lifetime – they had only been known to the Pietà.

And yet they were wonderful pieces – setting bright clarity against calm, as in so much of his music. No one until now had realized the passion and serenity of his religious works. Here was nothing of the histrionic bravura of the operas. A serenity hidden in the apparent worldliness of this strange priest, a religious energy and perception,

Above: Vivaldi is loved by both virtuosos and amateur musicians, experienced players and beginners alike. Opposite: The brilliant young violinist, Nigel Kennedy, who has introduced Vivaldi to thousands of people who had never heard his music. His recording of "The Four Seasons" made this classical piece rival the sales of pop music.

Music is forever young. Every generation rediscovers the masters. Vivaldi's experience at the Pietà enabled him to write wonderful music for every degree of skill. For many, he is the door to classical music.

shines through the splendid music.

With Antonio Vivaldi a way of life died. Thirty years after his death, the diary entry of a visitor to the Pietà reported, "the composition and performance I heard tonight did not exceed mediocrity." And yet the Pietà had fared better than the other Ospedali – where, by now, the music could be both inharmonious and inaccurate.

Outside the Ospedali there was an even greater deterioration of taste and performance, if contemporary observers are to be believed. The strange magic that had held Venice for so long was fading.

And yet Vivaldi himself, the red-haired priest, his grave lost under the traffic of Vienna, his music forgotten for two hundred years, reaches out of his own time to touch the hearts and minds of those who live today.

He would no doubt be delighted by his new success. And offering classes to the violin virtuosos of today.

Important Dates

1678   Mar 4: Antonio Lucio Vivaldi is born in Venice.

1693   Sept 18: Vivaldi, aged fifteen and a half, receives the tonsure, the first step to becoming a priest.

1703   Mar 23: Vivaldi, aged twenty-five, is ordained priest, but ill health prevents him from carrying out his duties for more than a year.
Sept: Vivaldi is appointed to teach the violin at the *Seminario musicale dell'Ospidale della Pietà*. His association with the Pietà lasts for forty years.

1705   Vivaldi's first published music appears: a collection of trio sonatas.

1708   Dec: The king of Denmark and Norway, Frederick IV, visits the Pietà. Before the king leaves Venice in March, Vivaldi presents him with a collection of twelve sonatas for violin and harpsichord.

1709   Feb: Vivaldi is voted out of office by the governors of the Pietà.

1711   Sept 27: Vivaldi, aged thirty-three, is re-appointed violin teacher at the Pietà.
Vivaldi's first set of concertos, *L'estro armonico*, is published.

1713   April: Vivaldi's first opera, *Ottone in Villa*, is performed in Vicenza.

1714   Vivaldi's first oratorio, *Moyses Deus Pharaonis*, is performed at the Pietà. *Orlando finto pazzo* is performed at the Teatro San Angelo in Venice. Vivaldi becomes involved in the management of the Teatro San Angelo, but withdraws after a year.

1715   Mar 6: Vivaldi meets an influential German, Johann von Uffenbach, who orders ten *concerti grossi* from him.

1716   Nov: Vivaldi's second oratorio, *Juditha triumphans*, is presented at the Pietà.

1717   Vivaldi leaves the Pietà and goes to Mantua, where he spends three years in the service of Prince Philip. It is perhaps during this period that Vivaldi meets the singer, Anna Girò.

1720   Vivaldi returns to Venice.
Dec: Benedetto Marcello's satirical book, *Il teatro alla moda*, appears. It damages Vivaldi's reputation and none of his operas appear in Venice for three years.

1723   Vivaldi re-establishes his links with the Pietà by supplying two concertos for the Feast of the Visitation. The Pietà's governors ask him to write two concertos for them every month.

1725   Dec: Vivaldi's *Il cimento dell'armonia e dell'inventione*, a collection of twelve concertos, is advertized in the Amsterdam Gazette. The opening four works are called *Le Quattro Stagioni* (The Four Seasons).

1735   Aug: Vivaldi, aged fifty-seven, returns to the Pietà as *Maestro de Concerti*.

1736   Vivaldi becomes involved in negotiations to stage two operas in Ferraro. His activities as a priest and his friendship with Anna Girò are brought into question. He is forbidden to enter the city and has to hand over production to a local man.

1739	In Ferrara, Vivaldi's opera, *Siroe, re di Persia*, is a failure. The management refuses to stage the second opera.
1740	Mar 21: Vivaldi writes a sinfonia and three concertos for a concert performed at the Pietá for the visit of the King of Poland and Elector of Saxony, Prince Frederick Christian. Later in the year, Vivaldi leaves the Pietá.
1741	July 28: Antonio Lucio Vivaldi, aged sixty-three, dies in Vienna. After his death, both he and his music vanish into obscurity.
1922	A list of Vivaldi's known work is published. It reveals that much of the composer's music is missing.
1927	The Turin National Library acquires a collection of music from the Collegio San Carlo in Monferrato. The collection contains fourteen volumes of Vivaldi's work, but the numbering shows that the collection is incomplete.
1930	The rest of the collection is found and acquired by the Turin National Library.
1939	A festival of Antonio Vivaldi's music is held in Siena, Italy. It is the start of a revival of interest in the composer and his work.

"As more and more collections of old music are acquired by libraries accessible to the researcher and the bibliographer one should expect a narrowing of the avenues of discovery. That this has not happened in Vivaldi's case is a testimony to his enormous productivity and the unusually wide circulation of his music in his lifetime."
   Michael Talbot, from his biography, "Vivaldi".

Recommended listening:
Violin Concerto: The Four Seasons; Spring, Summer, Autumn, Winter.
Bassoon Concerto: Night (for bassoon, string orchestra and continuo). The 1st movement describes dreams, the 2nd sleep, the 3rd dawn.
Oboe Concerto: Concerto in F major for oboe, string orchestra and continuo.
Concerto Grosso: Concerto for strings in G minor.
Choral Music: "Gloria" for 4 voices and orchestra.

Musical terms

Aria: In *opera*, originally a song for one or more voices, but now for a solo voice.

Cadenza: An improvised passage for a solo voice or instrument. The practice was first used by *opera* singers in the eighteenth century before the final part of an *aria*. Today, such improvisation is now very rare; the composer or performer writes their own cadenza beforehand, or uses an already published piece.

Cantata: In the seventeenth century, an extended piece of non-religious choral music for one or two voices with accompaniment. Since the eighteenth century, the term has been used to describe an extended piece of choral music with accompaniment. It can be either religious or non-religious, and with or without solo voices.

Concerto: Originally, a work for orchestra, usually with four *movements* and with or without solo instruments. Vivaldi revolutionized the concerto by giving prominence to a solo instrument and moving to the three-*movement* form that is in general use today.

Continuo: An important concept referring to an accompaniment written as a base line only, sometimes with numbers beneath each note. (This was also sometimes known as a figured bass.) This part was played by a keyboard player who interpreted the numbers to form chords. This allowed for a certain amount of creativity on the part of the player. The player "continued" through the whole piece, unlike most solo instruments.

Fugue: A composition for a given number of "voices" (instrumental or vocal), in which a melody is introduced by one "voice" and taken up and imitated by the others.

Libretto: The text of an *opera*.

Movement: A self-contained section of a large composition. Each section usually has its own key, tempo and structure. A large composition that does not have any such sections is described as being "in one movement".

Opera: A dramatic work in which all or most of the performers sing their parts. Opera, as it is known today, was first performed in Italy in the early 1600s. The first public opera house opened in Venice in 1637. Vivaldi's first opera was performed in Vicenza in 1713. In 1739, he claimed he had written ninety-four operas, but only forty-five are documented.

Oratorio: A semi-dramatic, musical work on a religious theme for chorus, soloists and orchestra. The term was originally used of musical services held at the Oratory of St. Philip Neri in Rome in the sixteenth century.

Recitative: A type of singing used for the narrative parts of an *opera*. Because of the freedom allowed in rhythm and pitch, such singing is associated with dramatic speech rather than song.

Sonata: Before 1750, the term used to describe a musical composition for a solo instrument, or one or more solo instruments with an accompaniment played from the bass line. Today, the term describes a composition, that is made up of several *movements,* for a solo instrument, or solo instrument and piano.

Sinfonia: Literally, a *symphony,* but in the seventeenth century, it was the term for an instrumental piece used as the introduction to an *opera*.

Symphony: Since the middle of the eighteenth century, a long composition, usually in the form of a *sonata* and made up of several *movements,* for orchestra. See also *sinfonia*.

Syncopation: The placing of an accent on a beat that is not normally accented, so that weak beats become strong and strong beats become weak.

Trio Sonata: This is actually a composition for four instruments – usually two violins, cello and harpsichord. The title refers to the three string instruments involved, as the composer wrote only three lines of music for them. The harpsichord player had to follow the cello line and improvise the harmonies.

Virtuoso: A performer with remarkable skill and technical expertise.

Index

Bach, Johann Sebastian 55, 56

Carnival 20-2, 25, 31
Catone in Utica 28, 49
La Constanza trionfante degl'amori e degl'odi 35

L'estro armonico 30

La Fenice 29
Ferrara project 47-52
Foa, Robert 57
The Four Seasons 42-4

Gasparini, Francesco 15
Gentili, Alberto 56
Giordano, Filippo 57
Giraud, Anna 39, 46, 47, 49, 51, 53
Goldoni 47

Juditha triumphans 35-8

Marcello, Benedetto 39
Monteverdi, Claudio 24
Moyses Deus Pharaonis 35

L'Olimpiade 46
Opera
  beginning of 24
  in Venice 27, 28-9
  interest in 24-5
Orlando finto pazzo 27
Ottone in Villa 25, 26

Pietà, The 12-14, 15-17, 52

Le Quattro Stagione 42-4

Siroe, re di Persia 51

Il Teatro alla moda 39-41, 44
Teatro San Angelo 27, 41, 45
Tito Manlio 38

Venice 8-10
  and Carnival 20-2, 25
  history of 6-7
  life in 18-19, 20
  musical heritage 7-8, 10
  and opera 27, 28-9
Vivaldi, Antonio
  birth 6
  death 53
  develops concerto 23, 30-2
  and Ferrara project 47-52
  first published music 17
  and The Four Seasons 42-4
  friendship with Anna Giraud 39, 46, 47, 49, 51, 53
  friendship with Goldoni 46-7
  ill health 12, 27, 38-9, 46, 53
  influence of 34, 43, 55-6
  legacy 59-61
  loses popularity 41, 45-6, 53-5
  in Mantua 38-9
  missing manuscripts of 56-7
  musical education 7, 11, 12
  musical output 17, 28, 29-30, 32-4, 38, 42, 44, 45, 46
  musical style 31-4, 35-7
  and The Pietà 12, 14-15, 23, 24, 38, 41, 47, 48-9, 52
  revival of interest in 55-7
  and *Teatro San Angelo* 27, 44-5
  trains for, and becomes priest 11-12
  travels of 41, 45
  as violinist 12, 17, 26, 30, 34
Vivaldi, Camilla Calicchio (mother) 5
Vivaldi, Giovanni (father) 5, 7, 10, 25, 41

This book is to be returned on or before...